How to Study and Learn

How to Study and Learn

by Janet Wikler

Illustrated by Tom Huffman
◂—*A First Book*—▸

Franklin Watts
New York / London / 1978

*For my father and mother,
and Arthur and Tara*

Library of Congress Cataloging in Publication Data

Wikler, Janet.
    How to study and learn.

  (A First book)
  Includes index.
  SUMMARY: Offers guidelines for improving learning and study skills such as taking tests and memorizing and suggests ways to deal with emotional interference.
    1. Study, Method of—Juvenile literature. [1. Study, Method of] I. Huffman, Tom. II. Title.
LB1049.W54   372.1′3′02812   77-15659
ISBN 0-531-01409-6

Copyright © 1978 by Franklin Watts, Inc.
All rights reserved
Printed in the United States of America
5 4 3 2 1

Contents

Feelings and Studying
1

How Do You Learn?
5

What Happens at School?
12

What Happens at Home?
22

Memorizing
31

Learning Concepts
38

Taking the Terror Out of Tests
49

Index
64

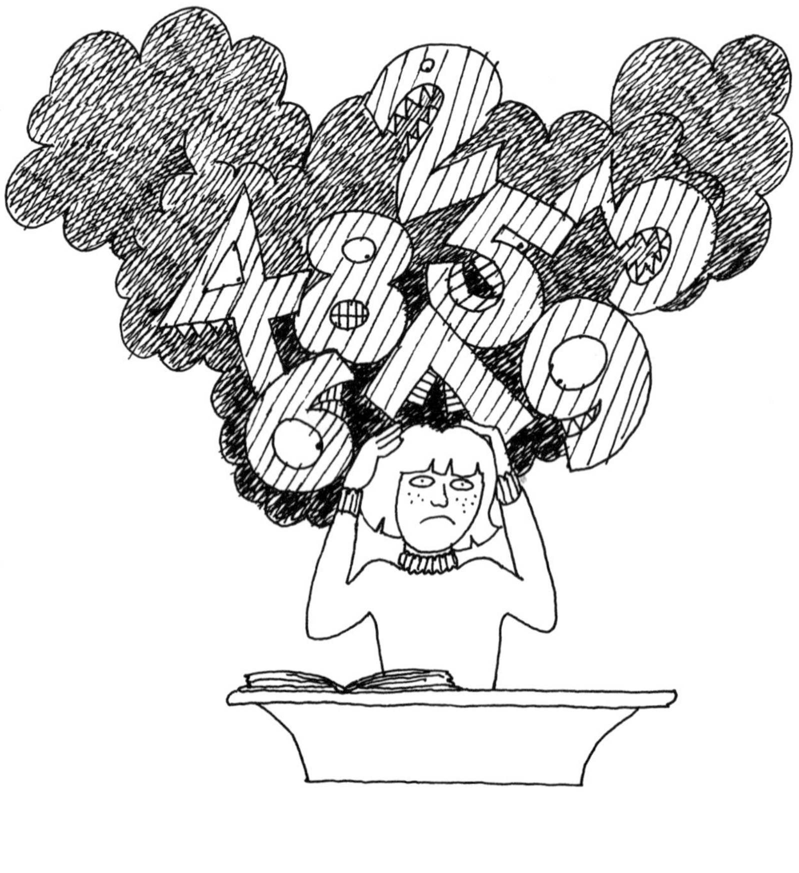

Feelings and Studying

Do you ever sit in class hoping your teacher won't call on you? Are you ever so worried that others will think you are "dumb" that you are afraid to ask a question in school?

Nearly everyone has had trouble understanding or remembering things in school. The truth is, there are no magic formulas, no shortcuts to learning. But there are habits you can develop to make school and learning easier. And there are a few simple ideas that can really help you feel better and do better as you learn.

WHAT HAPPENS WHEN YOU ARE AFRAID?

Nancy sat in class and heard her teacher's voice. Tears stung her eyes. She didn't understand the arithmetic they were learning now, and she was terrified her teacher would call on her. She tried to squeeze herself down and hide behind the boy who sat in front of her. She hoped the other kids wouldn't find out how "dumb" she really was.

Have you ever felt this way? Most of us have experienced

the feelings Nancy was going through. The truth is, Nancy was not "dumb." She didn't understand something, and felt bad because of it. Her real problem was *fear*. Nancy was so scared of others finding out what she didn't know, that she couldn't even pay attention to the teacher. As a result she became even more lost.

Being afraid makes it almost impossible to learn or remember anything. If you are too busy being scared, you can't pay attention to much else!

What would you do in Nancy's situation? Would you hide behind the person in front of you? Or would you raise your hand and ask the teacher to explain what you didn't understand?

In most situations—at school, at home, or anywhere—if you hide when you are afraid, you'll become even more afraid. If you are afraid to admit that you don't understand something, you'll never understand.

The best way to deal with fear is to face it, and to do what you are afraid to do. The worst possible thing that might happen can't be as bad as the feeling of fear itself.

If Nancy had raised her hand in class and told the teacher she was having trouble understanding the work, the teacher would have been happy to explain. That is what she was there for, after all! And the other kids would probably have been glad for Nancy's question.

But Nancy had not understood the arithmetic lessons for months, and she just couldn't admit that in front of the whole class. When she found herself feeling so bad and scared about it that she couldn't enjoy herself at all, she finally went to the teacher alone at the end of the school day. As soon as she asked for help, she began to feel a lot better. And once she finally caught up with the class, she learned to ask questions when she first had trouble with something, instead of waiting until she was months behind.

If there is something you don't understand in school, it's likely that others don't understand either. They will probably be grateful to you for asking a question—and admire your courage for doing it, as well.

If the thought of speaking up and asking for help in front of the others bothers you, then speak to your teacher alone, at recess or after school. Once you get up the courage to ask for the help you need, your battle is half won. You'll feel better, and with a little help, you'll soon catch up with your class.

THINGS TO THINK ABOUT

Try to remember a time when you didn't understand a topic that was being taught in school.

Which is smarter: to be quiet when you don't understand something, or to ask about it? Why? If somebody in your class asks a question, how do you feel? How do you think the others feel when you ask a question?

How Do You Learn?

Do you know how to swim? Can you throw and catch a frisbee? Do you remember writing your name for the first time? How did you feel? Skills don't develop like magic. They have to be learned.

Learning is a kind of problem solving. And solving the problem—learning whatever you set out to learn—is one of the most exciting feelings in life.

How does learning take place? Whether it is learning a sport or learning to read and write, all learning has certain steps in common.

WHAT DO YOU WANT TO LEARN?

The first step in problem solving—or learning—is naming the problem. This means you have to know what you want to learn. The better you understand your goal, the better your chance of reaching it. A goal like "doing well in school" is too general to be useful. It can be broken down into smaller goals, which are easier to work with. Some examples are: "learning to read better"; "learning to write better"; "improving your number skills"; and so on.

WHAT ARE THE STEPS INVOLVED?

Once you have decided what you want or need to learn, break it down into smaller steps. In swimming, for example, the steps might look like this:

1. learning to put my head in the water and hold my breath;
2. learning to float on my stomach with my head in the water;
3. learning to kick my legs while floating on my stomach with my head in the water;
4. learning to move my arms while kicking my legs, floating on my stomach with my face in the water;
5. learning to move my head from side to side and breathe while moving my arms, kicking my legs, and lying on my stomach in the water.

For a youngster learning to write her name for the first time, the steps might look like this:

1. learning to hold a pencil;
2. learning to spell my first name;
3. learning to spell my last name;
4. learning to write the letters in my first and last name.

For a student learning to write a book report, these steps are necessary:

1. learning to read and write;
2. learning to choose a book and reading it;
3. thinking about what I have read;
4. learning to pick out the main ideas in the book;
5. learning to organize the main ideas in order of importance;
6. learning to put the ideas into sentence and paragraph form.

Practically anything anyone learns in life is learned in steps. To learn something really well, you have to be sure of each step before going on to the next one. When you have learned every step and can put them together, your learning is complete.

Some new skills are learned by combining old skills. For example, if you already know how to add and subtract, and you know how many pennies, nickles, dimes, and quarters make a dollar, you can combine those skills in learning to make change at a store.

SKILLS CHART

Before learning a new skill, you have to know each step involved, and how to combine the steps. Asking yourself questions can help you name the steps. Practice can help you learn them and combine them.

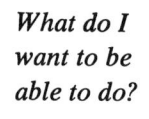

What do I want to be able to do?	*What skills do I need to do it?*
riding a bicycle with no training wheels	balance steering pedaling braking watching
writing a book report	reading writing spelling making sentences making notes picking out main ideas organizing ideas writing paragraphs
baking a cake	reading a recipe measuring ingredients mixing ingredients greasing a pan turning on the oven timing
playing the piano	fingering the keys reading music using pedals playing with my right hand playing with my left hand

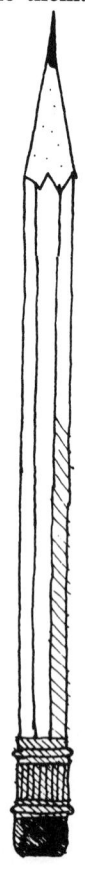

Which of these skills do I know already?	Which of the skills are new?	What separate skills do I need to combine?
steering pedaling watching	balance braking	all of them—balance, steering, pedaling, braking, watching
reading writing spelling making sentences	making notes picking out main ideas organizing ideas writing paragraphs	writing and spelling reading and taking notes making sentences and writing paragraphs picking out main ideas and organizing ideas
reading measuring mixing greasing a pan timing	turning on the oven	all of them
fingering the keys (right hand only) reading music playing with my right hand	fingering the keys (left hand) using the pedals playing with my left hand	combining the left and right hands with correct fingering reading music and playing notes reading music, playing notes, and using the pedals

HOW DO YOU LEARN EACH STEP?

Once you know what the steps are in the skill you want to learn, you need *practice* to learn each step. When you first started school, you learned to write the letters of the alphabet. You probably learned one letter at a time, and practiced writing it until it was easy. Then, you went on to the next letter, practiced it, and so on, until you knew the entire alphabet and could write every letter. Once you knew your letters, you could begin writing words. Again, you learned by practicing—writing each word you learned until you could do it easily.

WHAT HAPPENS IF YOU MISS A STEP?

There is a saying that a chain is only as strong as its weakest link. Even if there are a hundred links on a chain, if one is weak, the whole chain will break.

In the same way, if a building is strong but it is built on a weak foundation, the building will probably fall down. If you were making a building out of blocks, and one of the blocks at the bottom was weak and collapsed, the whole building would collapse.

Learning is the same way. Because learning any skill depends on practicing and combining a series of steps, if you leave out a step or don't bother to practice it until you know it well, you will not be able to learn the skill well. If you are not sure how to write all the letters, you are certain to have trouble writing words. If you never really learn the right way to kick while swimming, you'll never be a good swimmer. And if you don't understand the arithmetic lesson today, you won't be able to understand tomorrow's lesson either.

To really learn a skill, then, you need to learn one step at a time, practice, learn the next step, and combine them. You would not be able to run now if as a baby you had never learned to sit, to crawl, and to walk.

THINGS TO THINK ABOUT

Think of a skill that you cannot do now but would like to be able to do. Asking yourself the questions on the skills chart (page 8), write down the steps you think are involved.
1. Can you do any of these steps now?
2. Which steps do you think would be easiest? Why?
3. Which would be hardest? Why?
4. Are there any skills you already have that you could use in learning this one?

Write down the steps involved in learning the following skills (you can use the questions on the skills chart to help you):
1. taking photographs
2. reading
3. making change at a store

What Happens at School?

How do you feel at school? Are you restless? Do you speak up in class? You may listen to what the teacher and the other students are saying—or you may find your mind drifting off into daydreams, and miss what's going on. Do you think about what's happening right now, or what happened at home last night? Do you worry about what people are thinking of you? You probably have all these feelings sometimes, and others as well.

Most of us have lots of different thoughts and feelings during a whole school day. It is normal to have shifting thoughts and feelings over any period of time. But school is a special situation. There are times in school when really concentrating will help you learn a lot that you'll remember, and cut down on the amount of studying you'll need to do at home. And there are other times, like lunch and recess, that are especially made for letting your thoughts wander, for relaxing and playing.

PAYING ATTENTION PAYS OFF.

Tara stared out the classroom window, thinking of Halloween. The teacher's voice seemed like a faraway hum. She watched the yellow and orange leaves fall from the trees outside, dreaming of her Wonder Woman costume.

"Tara? Do you know the answer?" the teacher's voice broke sharply into her dreams. Tara realized she hadn't heard anything the teacher had said for the last few minutes. The other kids were looking at her, smiling at her confusion. She didn't even know what the question had been, and she felt embarrassed and angry.

Has this ever happened to you? Most of us have had times when we were not paying attention and didn't even realize it until someone asked us a question. Not only is it embarrassing to be caught daydreaming in school, but it makes it harder to understand the things your are learning.

Everyone has the power to pay attention. But it takes *wanting to pay attention,* and concentrating on what is going on. If there is something else going on in your mind when you should be paying attention in school, tell yourself you can think about it later. If you make yourself listen to what the teacher and the other kids are saying, you'll never get lost or be caught unaware.

**GETTING INTERESTED
IN THE SUBJECT HELPS.**

Do you have a favorite subject in school? What is it? Is there a subject you really dislike? Which one?

If you are like most of us, you do better in the subjects you like, and you probably pay better attention when working on those subjects in school. It's natural to pay attention to something that is interesting to you; and it's natural, too, to do well in something you pay attention to.

What is it you like about your favorite subject? What is it you don't like about your least favorite subject? You may find that you like a subject because you do well in it, or don't like a subject because it is hard for you.

Try an experiment tomorrow in school: treat the subjects you don't like as though they were your favorites. Really listen, and try to get interested. Chances are, you'll find that you really do get interested in a subject you thought you didn't like. Ask questions, and give your own opinions. You'll probably discover interesting ideas that you never had before. And you'll probably begin to understand better, and to do better work in the subject.

How do your feelings about a subject and your performance in that subject affect one another?

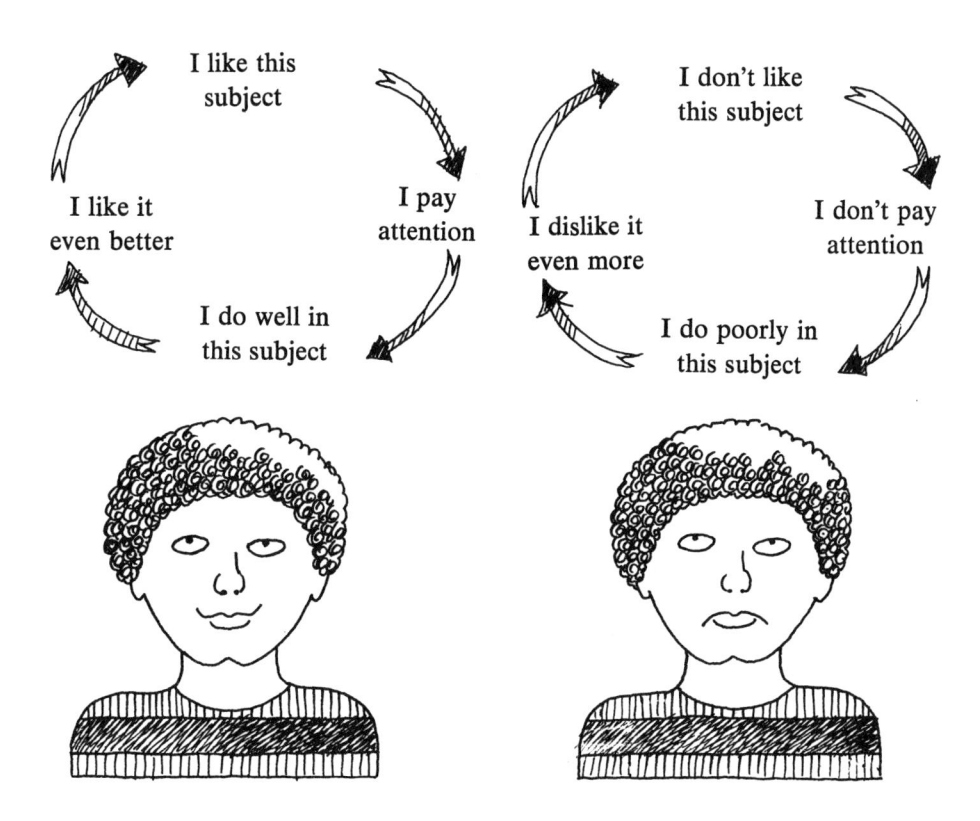

I like this subject → I pay attention → I do well in this subject → I like it even better

I don't like this subject → I don't pay attention → I do poorly in this subject → I dislike it even more

ASKING QUESTIONS HELPS YOU GET INTERESTED.

There is nothing as boring as sitting silently while someone talks on and on and on at you. Your teacher probably gets bored when she or he talks and no one asks questions or makes comments. Pretend you are teaching your teacher how to teach. Listen carefully, and think about whether she or he is explaining things clearly. When something seems unclear, it might be the teacher's teaching that is at fault, not your learning ability. If you are listening and you still don't understand something, raise your hand. Asking questions makes things more interesting for everyone. It will help you concentrate and listen and learn; it will help your teacher know how she or he is doing as a teacher; and it will help the others in your class understand what is going on.

**TAKING NOTES HELPS YOU
KNOW WHAT IS IMPORTANT.**

Have you ever tried to write down everything your teacher said, and given up because you couldn't write fast enough? Have you ever wished you had written down what your teacher said in class, because you couldn't remember and wanted to? Both these problems can be solved by good note-taking.

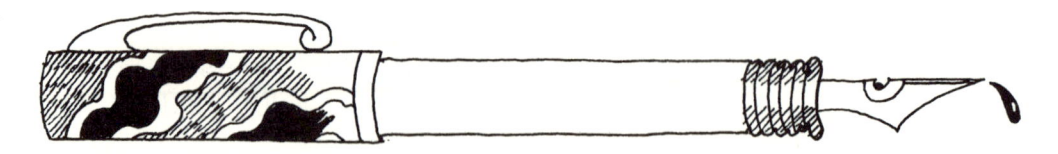

Don't try to write everything. Even if you could write everything your teacher said, you wouldn't have good notes. Part of taking notes is deciding what is important enough to write down, and what is not so important to remember. There are some things that act as clues to tell you when to write something down: when your teacher repeats something, it is probably important.

When she or he speaks slowly and says, "Now, this is important," it is a good idea to write it down. As you get to know your teacher better, you will know when what she or he is saying is important enough to write down, and when it is not.

Mr. Henry's fifth-grade class was studying American history. One day, Mr. Henry said: "The War of 1812 had three important results in the United States. First, the war helped to create a national spirit—a feeling of unity among the people of New England, the South, and the West. Before the war, these three regions of the country had had so many differences and conflicts that the United States had not really been 'united' at all. But in the years following the War of 1812, Americans began to forget their differences and turned their attention to building up a greater and stronger nation.

"The second result was the growth of manufacturing in this country. Before the War of 1812, most manufactured goods used by Americans were imported from other countries. But during the war, shipping was dangerous, and President Jefferson and the Congress placed an *embargo* on American shipping, to try and stop the European nations from capturing American ships. The Embargo Act of 1807 made it illegal for any American vessels to leave for foreign ports. So Americans had to manufacture their own goods, and they continued to do so after the war was over.

"The third result of the War of 1812 was the emergence of two new leaders, both outstanding generals who later became Presidents of the United States. These men were Andrew Jackson and William Henry Harrison."

Here are the notes of two of Mr. Henry's students:

Steve's notes:

War of 1812 — 3 imp. results in U.S.

1. National spirit — unity

2. Growth of U.S. manufacturing
   a. Shipping dangerous during war.
   b. Embargo Act of 1807 — Amer. ships could not leave for foreign ports so Americans had to manufac. their own goods — kept on after war

3. 2 new leaders — generals who become Pres
   a. Andrew Jackson
   b. William Henry Harrison

Andrew's notes:

The War of 1812 had 3 important results:

1. New England, South and West had conflicts

2. Shipping was dangerous and illegal

3. Outstanding generals became presidents

Whose notes are better, Steve's or Andrew's? Why? Which student's notes are going to mislead him when he tries to study for the test?

Your notes are your tools for making studying easier. Be good to yourself in making your own tools. Write clearly enough for you to read them easily later. Use abbreviations that you will be able to understand. Some simple abbreviations that are helpful are: "disc." for discovered; "imp." for important; and so on. Sometimes it's helpful to leave out little connecting words such as "the," "but," "a," and so forth. You don't have to use complete sentences, as long as you know what you mean, and can understand it when you read it over later.

YOUR HAND HAS A MEMORY.

Which way do you learn more easily: by reading something or by writing it? Scientists have found that the act of writing can help you remember something much better than you would by reading alone. It's as though your hand had a special connection with your eyes. If you write a sentence, then close your eyes, you can often see it just as it looked when you wrote it. It's almost as though your hand, by writing, were taking a photograph for your mind's eye to look at later.

Because of this, taking notes in school is a big step that can save you a lot of studying time at home. If you take notes during school, and then look over your notes at home in the evening, it will really help you remember, and you'll need to spend a lot less time reviewing before a test.

THINGS TO THINK ABOUT

When do you pay attention the best at school? When is it hardest for you to pay attention? Why?

Here are some reasons why people sometimes have trouble paying attention. Which of these reasons have kept you from paying attention in school sometimes? Can you think of other things that make it hard to pay attention?

1. being worried about something at home
2. being worried about what other kids think of me
3. not getting enough sleep the night before
4. being hungry
5. being uncomfortable (clothes too tight, having to go to the bathroom, not feeling well)
6. being afraid that I won't do well in the subject
7. thinking about something I am going to do later
8. talking to somebody else in class

What would be good ways of handling each of these problems? What happens in school when these things keep you from paying attention?

What Happens at Home?

WHERE TO STUDY

Look at the picture at the top of this page. If you have ever tried to study and watch television at the same time, the scene is probably familiar to you. What is the boy doing? How many things is he trying to do at once?

Barry lived with his mother, father, baby sister, and dog in a small apartment. He shared a room with his baby sister. The house was always noisy, with people talking, the TV on, the baby crying. When Barry tried to do his homework, something always seemed to interrupt him. It was hard for him to concentrate. Barry began to do poorly in school. He never seemed to have his homework done on time.

What would you do in Barry's situation? Would you try to do your homework in the middle of noise and confusion? Or would you talk things over with your parents, and ask them to help you create a study space for yourself?

Where you study is important. In front of the television is the worst possible place. You need enough light to read and write without straining your eyes. You need a flat surface, like

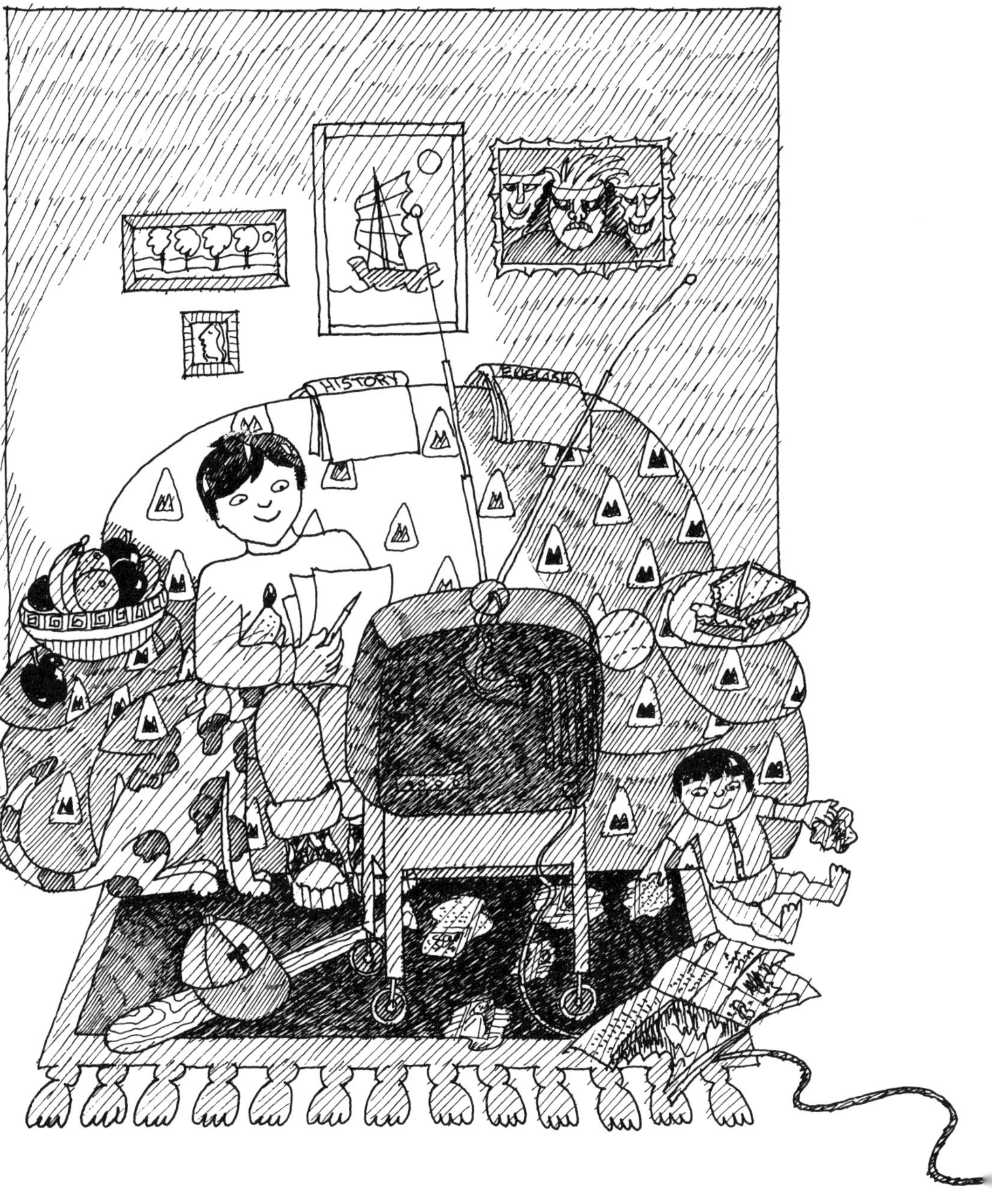
HISTORY
ENGLISH

a desk or a table, to work at. You and the rest of your family must understand that you have a right to a quiet, well-lighted place where you can do your homework.

Here are the things you need in order to study well:

1. a quiet place
2. a place to be alone
3. enough light
4. a flat table or a desk with a chair
5. sharp pencils and an eraser
6. paper
7. whatever books you will be using
8. a dictionary

Here are the things that can make it impossible to learn:

1. trying to learn with the TV on
2. not enough light
3. too much noise
4. people around, especially if they are talking to you
5. no flat surface to write on (it is hard to write neatly or clearly if you are leaning on something soft, like your lap)
6. no supplies around (pencil, paper, eraser, books)

Use this as a checklist when you get ready to do your homework. The idea is to make sure you have the right conditions *before* you begin.

YOU HAVE RIGHTS AS A STUDENT.

If you have trouble creating the right space for yourself to study in, speak to your parents about it. Every student has the right to a good study space. If you still can't create the right space after speaking to your parents, try studying in a school or public library. Having the right conditions for studying can double your learning in half the time.

WHEN TO STUDY

"I don't feel like it now; I'll do it later."
"It's too late; I'll do it tomorrow."
"I forgot. I'll do it after the next program is over."
"Do I *have* to? Now?"

Do these sentences sound familiar? How many times have you decided to put off until tomorrow something you did not feel like doing today? And how many times have you found that the next day, you have twice as much work and still don't feel like doing it?

It is natural for people to feel like putting off something they don't feel like doing. But putting things off just makes them pile up, and then doing them is much worse.

The first time Katie's mother asked her to clean up her room, Katie said, "Not now; another time." Every day, her mother asked her to clean up her room, and every day, Katie said, "Another day."

One day, Katie wanted to invite her friend Nina to sleep overnight at her house. Her mother agreed. Katie decided it was time to clean up her room. By this time, the room was so messy that the job took Katie nearly three hours. If she had done it a little bit at a time, every day, it would probably have taken her fifteen minutes at the most.

On Monday, Amy's teacher told the class there would be a test on Friday. The test would cover the four chapters in unit two of the science book.

"If you study one chapter a night," said the teacher, "you will have plenty of time to prepare."

On Monday night, Amy sat down to study, but her friend called on the phone, and after talking for half an hour, Amy decided it was too late to work. On Tuesday night, Amy decided to watch her favorite television shows instead of reading over the chapters of her book. On Wednesday, Amy played softball with some other kids on her block until dark. After that, she decided she was too tired to study. On Thursday night, Amy sat down with her science book. She only had time to read two chapters before she had to go to bed. On Friday, Amy was afraid to go to school, and tried to get her parents to let her stay home. But they told her she had to go to school, so she went and took the science test. How do you think she felt? How do you think she did on her test? Why?

How is cleaning up your room like doing your homework? How is it different? What happens if you put off doing your homework until the night before a test?

MAKING A STUDY SCHEDULE

Do you usually brush your teeth before you go to bed? Why? Is there anything else you do at a certain time each day? Eat lunch? Go to bed?

Most people have certain routines they follow—things they do every day, usually at the same time. These things become *habits,* and after awhile, they are just part of everyday life.

Making homework a part of your daily routine—as much a part as brushing your teeth or eating lunch—is one way of taking the pain out of it. If you set aside a certain time each day for doing homework, then at other times of the day you don't have to worry about your homework, and when it is time to do it, you will do it almost automatically.

Some people find that doing their homework as soon as they come home from school is good for them. These people like to get it off their minds early, so they can spend the rest of the evening in play and relaxation.

Others find that taking a break after school until dinner, and doing their homework right after dinner works well for them. Then, after their homework, they spend the rest of the evening relaxing until bedtime.

Whether you decide to set aside an hour or so every day after school, or do it right after dinner, here are a few tips that may help you do your homework more easily:

1. Never try to work hard when you are very hungry. If you decide to do your homework right after school, you may want to have a little snack before getting to work.
2. Always do your homework before you get too tired. Don't wait until very late in the evening, or the assignment will seem much harder than it really is.
3. Break your time up into manageable chunks. If you have more than an hour's work, give yourself a break after an hour. On the other hand, don't break it up so much that you can't get anything done—you should be able to work at least a half an hour at a time without stopping.
4. Don't put it off until the last minute. If you put off doing your homework, you will have it on your mind, and you won't enjoy your free time as much. If you put it off until the end of the week or until right before a test, you will have too much catching up to do for you to really learn. A little bit each night, enough to keep up with what is happening each day in school, will take the scare out of tests and keep you on top of it all.
5. Do your homework at the same time every evening. This will help you make it a habit—part of your daily routine. It will make it easier to do, and it will make your free time more enjoyable, as well.

SOME SAMPLE STUDY SCHEDULES

	3:30–4:30	4:30–5:30	5:30–6:30	6:30–7:30	7:30–8:30	8:30–9:30
Tara	come home; snack; play baseball	play baseball; come in and set table	eat dinner	write book report	do arithmetic	watch TV; go to bed
Liza	come home; read social studies	practice piano	play with puppy; visit neighbor	eat dinner	read book for book report	take bath; go to bed
Joshua	come home; snack; watch TV	read science chapter	study spelling	eat dinner	help with dishes	work on model airplane; go to bed
Andrew	come home; plant flowers in back yard	play with best friend	eat dinner	work on science project	work on science project	eat snack; go to bed

How would you make a schedule like this for yourself?

THINGS TO THINK ABOUT

What times of day do you feel best? Do you think these would be good times to do your homework? Why or why not?

Have you ever tried to work or study when you were very tired? How did you feel? How good was the work you did? How well did you remember what you studied? Why do you think this is so?

Have you ever tried to study while watching TV? How did it affect your work? How did it affect your enjoyment of TV?

Have you ever put something off until it was too late to do it? Why? What would you do now?

Memorizing

Can you put the missing words into the following sentences?

"You deserve a break today, at ———!"
"Have it ——— way at Burger King."
"Pop, pop, fizz, fizz, oh, what a ——— it is!"
"Things go better with ———."
"Hold the pickles, hold the ———, special orders don't upset us."

What other slogans have you memorized from commercials? Why do you think people learn advertising slogans?

Can you fill in these blanks?

"Rich man, poor man, beggarman, ——— ..."
"She'll be coming round the ——— when she comes."
"I've been working on the ——— all the livelong day."
"Thirty days has ———, April, June, and November."

Why do you think you know the answers? How did you *memorize* these songs and sayings?

PRACTICE MAKES PERFECT.

You probably practiced singing songs before you learned them. You practiced the commericals you remember, too—without even knowing it! One way advertisers get people to buy things is by repeating the same commercial so many times that people can't help remembering what they say. The people who write advertising know that the best way to *memorize* something—to learn to repeat it from memory—is by hearing it and saying it again and again and again. The advertisers know something else about remembering, too. It's easier to remember something when it makes sense to you, or when it has a rhyme or a rhythm to help link words to each other. When you have something you want to remember, if you can turn it into a piece of "advertising" or a "song," you will have clues to help you remember.

Larry found that making up rhymes could help him remember important dates in history: "In 1588, the Spanish

Armada met its fate." When the question appeared on the test, he remembered the rhyme he had made up while studying, and he got the answer right.

Nicole remembered a language arts lesson by making up a rhyme. "An adjective describes a noun; examples are 'big', 'good', and 'brown'."

Andrew remembered an important fact from a science lesson in this way: "When an apple fell from its tree, Newton discovered gravity."

Rhyme, rhythm, and song are all "clues" you can use to help you remember something. Often, you'll find you can make up your own rhymes, songs, or "commercials" to help you remember something you are learning in school.

MAKING SENSE OUT OF NON-SENSE

Look at the following two lists. Close your eyes and try to repeat each list. Which is easier to learn?

I.
apple
baby
cat
dog

II.
bock
ander
brin
yadrow

For most people, list I is much easier. It consists of real words that make sense. In addition, the four words begin with the first four letters of the alphabet, A, B, C, and D—another clue for remembering.

If you look again at the second list of "words," however, you will see that the first letters are B, A, B, and Y—spelling BABY. Now, you have one clue to help you memorize the list.

Jacob's mother asked him to go to the supermarket. "I need apples, milk, lemons, cheese, and eggs," she said. "Shall I write it down for you?"

"No," said Jacob. "I have a way of remembering." And he did. He took the first letter of each word, and rearranged them so they made a new word. By remembering the new word, he could remember the five things, one at a time, by remembering the first letter of each. What do you think was the new word that Jacob remembered? The answer is upside down at the bottom of this page.

Any time you have to memorize a list of words, take the first letter of each word in the list, and make a new word. Even a make-believe word that you can remember will help you think of the original words in the list.

TAKE A PICTURE WITH YOUR HAND.

Remember how we said the hand was the "camera of the mind"? This is especially true when it comes to memorizing. If you write something down that you want to remember, you will learn it much faster and remember it much better than if you simply read it and repeat it.

[34]

[Answer: Camel.]

It is also easier to remember something if you understand it. If you have to memorize a saying or a poem, and there are words you don't understand, look up those words before you try to memorize anything.

MEMORIZING IS PROBLEM SOLVING.

For her social studies class, Tara had to memorize the Preamble to the Constitution of the United States. It looked like this:

We, the people of the United States, in order to form a more perfect union, establish justice, insure domestic tranquillity, provide for the common defense, promote the general welfare, and secure the blessings of liberty to ourselves and our posterity, do ordain and establish this constitution for the United States of America.

First, Tara looked up the words she didn't understand. Then, she broke it into "bite-sized" pieces of three or four words each. Now, she read each piece, closed her eyes, repeated it, and tried to write it. When she could write one "piece," she went on to the next, until she could write every "piece" and put it all together.

By writing it with her hand, she helped to "take a picture" for her mind. Then, by "reading it back" from the "picture," she was able to write it from memory.

When going from one "piece" of learning to the next, always repeat what you have already learned before adding the next piece. That way, you are building on a firm foundation, and the learning will stay in your memory for a long time.

When Tara grew up, she won one thousand dollars on a game show for remembering the Preamble to the Constitution, which she had memorized when she was in fourth grade!

RULES CAN SOMETIMES HELP.

Sometimes, learning a general "rule" can help you learn things and remember them. For example, Steve had trouble with spelling. He tried to memorize the spelling of assigned words every week, but he had trouble. He never knew when a letter was doubled in a word, and when it was not.

Steve asked Andrew to help him. These were the words he was trying to spell:

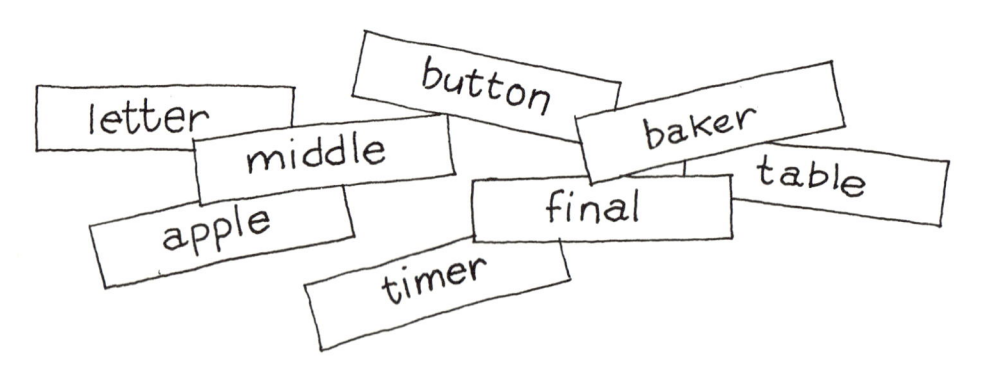

letter button baker middle table apple final timer

Andrew explained that when the vowel sound of the word was short, the consonant was usually doubled, and when the vowel sound was long, the consonant was usually single. Learning this spelling rule helped Steve a lot. Now, he had a clue to help him remember the correct spelling of the words.

Another spelling "rule" of this kind is: "I before E, except after C, or when sounding like A, as in *neighbor* and *weigh*."

[36]

THINGS TO THINK ABOUT

Write two lists: one, a list of words that have something in common (like all names of food, or all pieces of clothing); and one, a list of "made-up" words. Try to learn each list. Which is easier to remember? Why? What "tricks" can you figure out to help you remember the second list?

Make up a rhyme for a fact you are learning in school. Do you think you will still remember your rhyme and the fact in the rhyme a year from now? Why or why not?

Learning Concepts

USING YOUR MIND

Laura slept in the upper berth of the bunkbed; her younger sister Liza slept in the lower. Every night, Laura would complain to her mother, "It's so hot in here!" Here sister would say, "It is not! It's just right! Laura, how can you possibly think it's hot?"

Laura wondered why she and her sister could never agree on the right temperature for their room. If she was comfortable, her sister was cold; if Liza was comfortable, Laura sweated all night. She supposed it was just one of the mysteries of life.

One day, during a science lesson, Laura's teacher took two bowls filled with water and measured their temperatures. They were the same.

"Now," said the teacher, "I am going to put one bowl on the floor, over here. The other bowl, I am going to put on a shelf high up near the ceiling. Tomorrow morning, we'll take the temperature of the water in each of the bowls again. We'll see whether how high they are affects the water temperature."

The next morning, the class found that the water in the bowl near the ceiling was warmer than the water in the bowl near the floor.

The teacher explained why. "Warm air rises," he said, "because it weighs less than cold air. So, the air near the ceiling of a room will usually be warmer than the air near the floor."

That night, Laura was too hot to sleep very well, but at least she understood why. She was able to use her head to *generalize*—to take a concept she learned in school and understand something about her own life better because of it. This is the real purpose for most of the things people learn in school—to help them use their knowledge in their lives.

What concepts have you learned in school that you could generalize to other things in your life? What concepts have you learned outside of school that could help in school?

READING FOR REMEMBERING

Do you read all books in the same way? Do you think about what you are reading while you are reading it? Or do you wait until you have finished, then try to remember it all?

Reading for remembering takes more than just forcing your eyes across the pages of a book. To remember what you read, you need to think about it while you are reading it. Reading is a lot like listening: paying attention pays off. If you don't pay attention to what you read, you may as well not bother to do it at all.

TAKING NOTES HELPS YOU REMEMBER.

Just as taking notes in class helps you remember what goes on in class, so taking notes as you read will help you remember what you have read. You can use the clues in your book about what is important to decide which things to write in your notes, and which to pass over.

Here are two different examples of student notes on a section of the book *Dogs and Puppies* by Jane Rockwell (New York: Franklin Watts, 1976). Which notes are better? Why?

Housetraining. *Put newspapers around the puppy's bed to encourage paper training. Do not line the bed with newspapers or place them under the bed's rug or blanket. Your puppy must distinguish between bed, which is for rest, and newspapers, which are for another more immediate function!*

If the pup heads for the newspapers and uses them, praise it and give it a treat. If it is about to squat somewhere other than the papers, quickly pick it up and place it on the papers. If the puppy relieves itself where the papers aren't, say "no" in a firm voice and bring it to the papers with some encouraging words. Next, mop up the mistake with paper towels and use soda water or a deodorizer (available in most pet stores) to eliminate the odor. Remember, your puppy is learning. Loud, harsh words will frighten, not educate, it.

Housetraining generally is a fairly simple job. But there are exceptions! My dachshund, Jamie, was a demon to housetrain. He had more than the usual amount of dachsie stubbornness, plus the deviltry of most puppies. At the time, I was recuperating from an automobile accident. Try to keep up with and discipline a puppy when you're on crutches! Of course, I can't blame Jamie. He seemed to think it was all a very funny game. Finally, very reluctantly, I gave Jamie to the neighbors, who had a female dachshund and two teenagers. I knew they would provide my headstrong puppy with a loving home and the training he needed at the crucial time. Besides, they were a lot faster on their feet! [p. 36]

Jennifer's notes:

Housetraining

1. Put newspapers around the bed
2. Do not line the bed with newspapers or place them under the bed's rug or blanket
3. Your puppy must distinguish between bed for rest and newspapers for another important function
4. If the puppy uses the newspapers give it a treat
5. Mop up the mistake with a paper towel
6. Remember your puppy is learning
7. Jamie the dachshund was a demon to train
8. Try to keep up with a puppy when you're on crutches

Claudia's notes:

Housetraining
I. Newspapers
  A. Put around the bed but not in it or on it.
  B. When puppy uses newspapers, praise it & give it a treat.
  C. When puppy begins to squat somewhere else, quickly pick it up & place it on papers.
    1. If puppy makes mistake say "no" & bring it to papers with kind words — not harsh
    2. Mop up mistake with paper towels and use soda water or a deodorizer.
  D. Most puppies are easy to train but not all.

YOUR BOOKS GIVE YOU CLUES.

Books about school subjects—textbooks—are different from storybooks, and need to be read differently for you to get the most out of them. With a storybook, you can usually go right through and know what is going on. Even if you forget the details, you will remember the story line.

With textbooks, you will want to remember some of the details. One way of remembering is to think about what you are reading as you are reading it. Stop from time to time to consider what you have read, before going on to the next section or chapter. Like problem solving, learning from a book can best be accomplished by making sure you have mastered or digested one "piece" before going on to the next.

Take out a book you use in one of your school subjects, and look at how it's organized. Are there units? Chapters? Chapter sections? Chapter summaries? Review questions? Why do you think the book is organized in this way?

Most textbooks are organized in *units,* which deal with general themes. Examples would be, in science: Weather; Electricity; Space Exploration; and so on. In social studies, units might include: The Explorers; The Early Settlers; The Thirteen Colonies; The American Revolution; and so on.

Within each unit are one or more *chapters,* each of which deals with a particular theme. A unit on Weather, for example, might include chapters on rain and snow, temperature and humidity, and weather forecasting. A unit on the Thirteen Colonies might include chapters on the New England colonies, the Middle Atlantic colonies, and the Southern colonies. In this way the organization of your book tells you something about the subject, and can help you organize your thinking and your notes.

Each chapter usually consists of *sections,* often headed by sentences in bold-face type (**this is bold-face type**). The bold-face type is the author's way of saying, "This is important—a main idea to remember." A chapter about the New England colonies, for example, might include a heading like this: "Roger Williams founds Rhode Island." This heading gives you a clue about the information that follows in the text below.

Within each chapter section are one or more *paragraphs.* Every paragraph has its own organization, which will help you pick out the most important ideas for your notes. The first sentence, or "topic sentence," tells the main idea of the paragraph. Under the chapter heading in your notes, indent, and write the topic sentence of each paragraph. Sometimes, when there are important dates, names, or lists within a paragraph, you will want to include these in your notes as well. Often, the topic sentence will warn you when such names, dates, or lists are about to follow, with phrases like: "There are five major reasons why . . ." or, "Two men were influential in . . ." or, "The years immediately following the war were. . . ."

The last sentence in a paragraph will often sum up the major points made in the paragraph, and will give you a checkpoint for finding out whether you have understood what you read.

As you read, when you come across words or phrases you don't understand, always look them up in a dictionary or ask someone what they mean. It is almost impossible to learn something you don't understand.

Most textbooks have *summaries* and *review questions* at the end of every section or chapter. The summaries usually contain the most important information in the chapter, stated briefly. The summaries are provided to help you discover how well you have understood the chapter. Check each chapter summary against your notes, to make sure your notes contain everything in the chapter summary. (Sometimes your notes may include a little more detail; but everything in the summary is important and should be in your notes.) If there is something in a chapter summary that you don't understand or remember, you need to go back and read that part of the chapter again. Most of the things in a chapter summary are likely to appear on a test.

When you come to the review questions, try to write the answers without looking back. Remember that your hand is the camera of your mind. When you can write all the answers to the questions from memory, you will know you have learned the important things in the chapter.

YOUR READING NOTES WILL CUT YOUR STUDYING TIME.

Why should you bother to take notes while you read? Isn't it enough just to read the material? Can't you learn simply from reading each chapter through?

While you can learn something from reading without writing, you can learn a lot more and remember better when you write down important facts as you come to them. In addition to helping you remember, taking notes when you read will create an organized outline of the material in the book that will save you time later, when you review for a test. If you follow the book's organization in your notes, you will have a ready-made outline to use as a study tool. And you will be able to study from your class notes and your book outlines, without having to read every word in each chapter over again.

KEEP YOUR NOTES TOGETHER IN ONE PLACE.

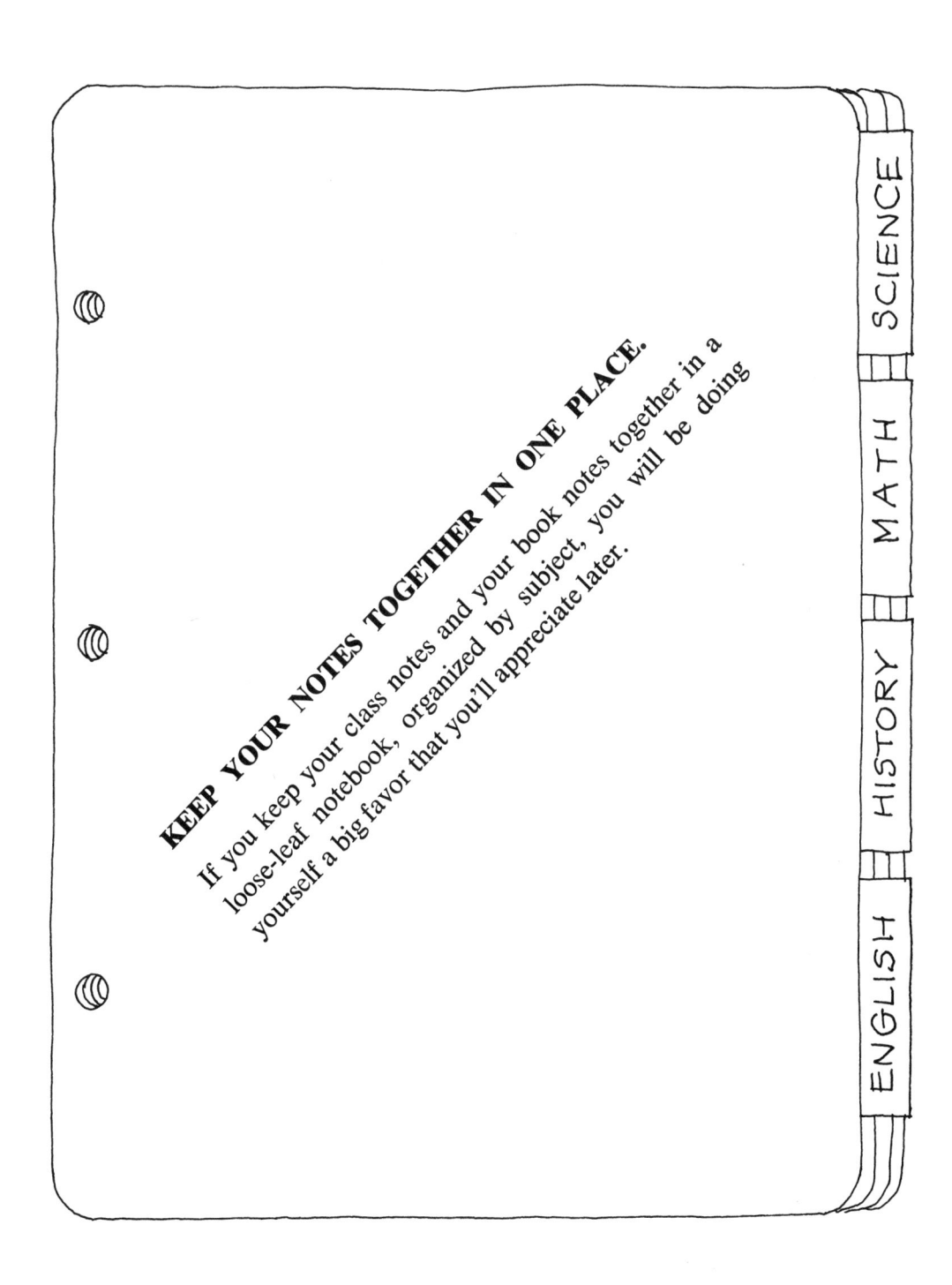

If you keep your class notes and your book notes together in a loose-leaf notebook, organized by subject, you will be doing yourself a big favor that you'll appreciate later.

THINGS TO THINK ABOUT

1. What is a concept you have learned in school this year? How has learning this concept helped you to understand something else?
2. What is the difference between reading a textbook and reading a storybook?
3. What should you write in your notes when you are reading a textbook? Which clues in the book tell you to pay special attention?
4. Why does writing the answers to review questions at the end of a chapter help you know how well you have learned the chapter contents? Do you think answering the questions without writing the answers is as useful? Why or why not?

Taking the Terror Out of Tests

"Next week, class," said Mr. Miller, "we will have a test on unit three."

Dead silence filled the room. Richard felt his heart begin to race. His palms were sweating. Tears filled his eyes, making the room look blurry. He hoped he could keep the tears from spilling over his eyelids and down his cheeks. He wished he could run out of the room, far away from school, and hide somewhere where nobody could find him.

How do you feel when your teacher announces a test? Do you feel panicky, like Richard? Do you wish there were some way you could avoid the whole thing? Do you long for a world where there are no tests at all?

Why do you think teachers give tests? And why are students afraid of them? Just thinking about these questions can be the first step in overcoming test terror.

TEST TERROR IS CONTAGIOUS.

One reason many students are afraid of tests is because their friends and classmates are afraid. Fear is *contagious*—"catching,"

like a cold or the flu. Like any feeling, fear isn't always based on reason. And there is no reason why anyone has to be afraid of tests.

WHY DO TEACHERS GIVE TESTS?

There are three main reasons why teachers give tests. First, the test results show the teacher how well he or she is doing as a teacher. If the whole class does poorly on a test, the fault probably lies with the teacher. If a whole class does well, the teacher knows that she or he has done a good job. And if some do well and some do poorly, the teacher can tell which students are having trouble with the subject, and need additional help.

The second reason why teachers give tests is to help each student see how well she or he has learned the material—and which parts of the subject the student may need to go over again. It's a way for you to measure your progress in a subject—and a way for you to catch any problems you may have before you fall too far behind.

The third reason—which is often the only reason the students think about—is to give the teacher a basis for grading or marking the students in her or his class. In many classes, the boys and girls worry so much about this aspect of testing that they forget about the other useful purposes that regular testing can serve.

BEING PREPARED

How do you prepare for a test? Do you wait until the night before, then try to learn everything all at once? Do you get together with your best friend and ask each other questions? Or do you start reviewing your classroom notes and reading notes a few days before the test?

If you do your homework regularly, and follow the suggestions for learning that are offered throughout this book, you will need to do very little extra studying before a test. *It is the day-to-day school and home learning that really prepares someone to do well on a test.* Last-minute "cramming" can never substitute for studying a little bit each day. It takes time to learn, and that includes time between learning sessions. It simply cannot be done all at once, in a hurry.

WHAT HAPPENS WHEN YOU "CRAM"?

Melanie found out on Wednesday that her class was going to have a test on Monday covering a social studies unit the class had been working on for a month. She had done some of the reading, but not all of it. When she had written homework, she'd done it while watching TV—not really concentrating on it, just doing it so she'd have something to turn in.

On Sunday night, Melanie decided to study for her test. It covered three chapters, each of which was about fifteen pages long. She started reading the chapters, and found it took longer than she had thought it would. She began to panic, and to try to read faster. But the more she panicked and the faster she read, the less she found she could remember. There seemed to be so many little facts! She tried putting her book aside and reading over her classroom notes. The handwriting was messy, and at times, when her mind had been wandering during class, she hadn't bothered to take any notes at all.

At ten o'clock, when her parents told her she had to go

to bed whether she was finished or not, Melanie had read only one of three chapters, and her messy, incomplete classroom notes. She had trouble getting to sleep that night, and lay in bed, shivering with fear.

How do you think Melanie did on her test? If you think she did poorly, you're right. There was no way that Melanie could learn in one night all the things she was supposed to be learning for a month. She had to learn the hard way what happens when you "cram."

STUDYING ALONE AND STUDYING TOGETHER

Michael decided, when he heard about the test, to ask his friend Peter to study with him. Peter was smart, and Michael figured that even though he hadn't kept up with his daily work, Peter could teach it all to him in a night.

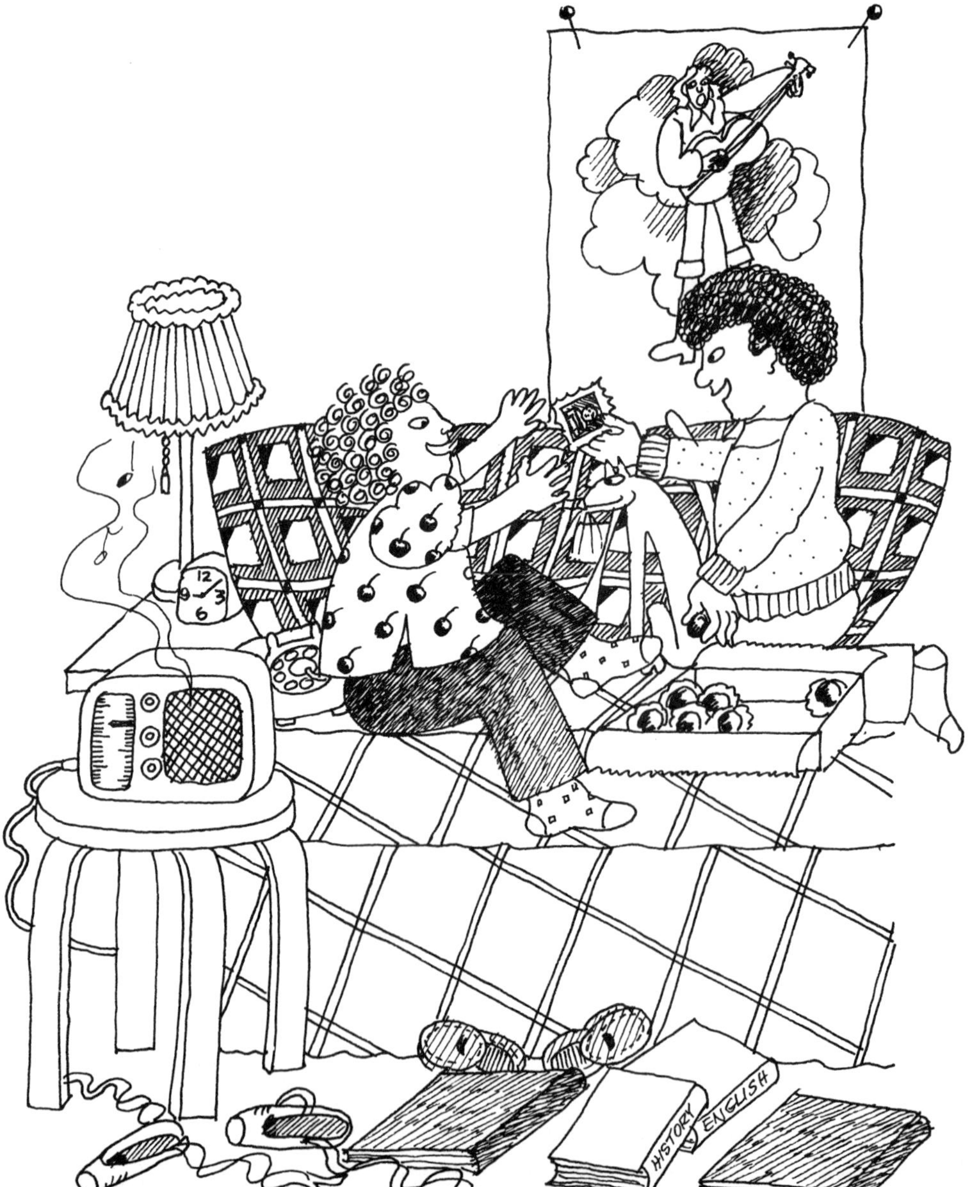
HISTORY
ENGLISH

Peter had done his homework every night, and had taken notes while reading his textbook. He had listened in class, too, and had good notes. He came over to Michael's house the night before the test, and tried to teach Michael everything he had learned.

What do you think happened? Peter, who already knew the subject, learned it even better by trying to teach it. But Michael, even though he listened to what Peter was saying, couldn't remember it all. It was just too much to learn in a night.

Studying together only works when the two (or more) people who are studying together already know the material well. If you have kept up with your daily reading and homework assignments, and have listened in class, it can help you remember what you already know if you tell it to someone else. If you both know the material, you can ask each other questions and compare notes. But if only one of you has learned the material, only the one who already knows the subject will benefit from studying together. The one who hasn't done the work simply can't learn it all in one or two nights.

HOW TO MAKE SURE YOU ARE PREPARED

The only way to be really sure you're prepared to take a test and do well on it is to follow the suggestions given throughout this book. Keep up on a daily basis with what you're learning in school. Take good notes, both in class and while reading at home. If you've done all this, then all you need to do when you learn there is going to be a test is to read carefully over your notes, the chapter summaries in your book, and the review questions in your book. You will probably find, if you have kept up, that most of the material is familiar to you, and that you can answer most of the review questions.

WHEN TO BEGIN STUDYING FOR A TEST

Of course, if you are keeping up with your work, you are always studying for a test. That's why keeping up means less last-minute studying. But even if you have kept up and done your classwork and your homework every day, you will probably want to do some extra reviewing for a few days before you take the test.

Start going over your notes about three days before the test. Read them over carefully—both your classroom notes and your reading notes—and see if there is anything there that you don't understand. If so, read that part of your book again, or ask your teacher to explain that part of the material.

After you've finished reviewing your notes, read the chapter summaries for the chapters that will be covered in the test. Some students find that making up tests for themselves from the chapter summaries—writing down the questions and then writing the answers without looking at the text—really helps them remember the material. Whether or not you make up a "test" from the chapter summaries, try to answer all the review questions at the end of each chapter. And remember to answer them in *writing,* not just in your head—"the hand is the camera of the mind," and writing the answers will help you remember them when the same questions—or similar ones—appear on the test.

THE NIGHT BEFORE

What do you do the night before a test? Do you spend long hours trying to memorize last-minute names, dates, and facts? Do you stay up as late as possible, denying yourself any fun, so you can learn everything there is to know?

It may surprise you to find out that the best students don't behave this way at all. If you've kept up with your work all along, and have started reviewing your notes and book several days before the test, then the best thing you can do the night before the test is to get yourself into a relaxed frame of mind, and get a good night's sleep. You will probably want to spend about an hour going over the chapter summaries one last time, and reading your notes again; but an hour's studying should be plenty if you've kept up all along. By the night before the test, either you know it or you don't. And long hours of frantic "cramming" will only make you panicky, exhausted, and too scared, frightened, and confused to remember what you really do know.

So, that last night before a test, be good to yourself. After one last overall review, take a warm bath, relax, and go to bed early. The best thing you can do at this point is to make sure your mind and body are in top condition.

THE DAY OF THE TEST

When you wake up the day of the test, don't try to cram last-minute facts into your head. That kind of studying is more confusing than helpful. Get up, get dressed, and—this is important—*eat a good breakfast!* Your brain needs nourishment if you're going to do your best.

When you get to school, don't join the knot of frantic students that always seems to congregate just before a test. The last-minute questions that students ask each other only build the panic level and make everyone afraid. If you don't know it by now, that scared little group isn't going to help you learn it.

NOTHING TO FEAR BUT FEAR ITSELF

The most important thing to remember before and during a test is to *keep calm*. Fear can keep your mind from working as well as it should. When you get to your classroom, sit down in your seat and wait for the test to begin. Try to think of pleasant, non-test related things. A relaxed frame of mind can make an enormous difference in how well you are able to perform on a test.

No single test is going to make or break your grade. Teachers grade on the basis of more than one test, and on classroom performance and participation as well. So, do as well as you can, and that is all anyone can ask. If you keep to yourself right before the test, rather than clustering and talking with the other students, you will probably stay calmer and do much better than they will.

TAKING THE TEST

All right—the moment has arrived. The talking stops. The teacher passes out the papers. The test has begun. How do you feel? What do you do?

It's natural to feel some fear; but try to keep it in proportion. The kind of fear you feel in a horror movie doesn't keep you from doing whatever you want to do, because you know it is not going to have any long-term effect on your life. One test isn't going to have a long-term effect on your life, either. It takes a lot of tests to make a lasting mark.

Instead of letting fear get in the way, concentrate on sizing up the test as a whole. Before you do anything else, write your name on your paper. Then read over all the questions—before you answer any of them. This will give you a good idea of how long the test is, and how hard it is in general. It will help you to *pace* yourself—to know how much time to spend on each part of the test.

If you have a watch, wear it. If you don't, try to borrow one or bring a small clock with you to class; or use the clock that is hanging in the classroom. Try and make sure you don't spend so much time on one question or one section that you don't have time for the others.

After you have looked over the test as a whole, go back to the beginning again. Now, try to answer the questions you are sure you know. Go through the whole test, answering each question you know, and lightly marking those you don't know or aren't sure of.

After you have answered all the questions you're sure of, go back to the beginning again. Now, do the checked questions—the ones you are not sure of—one at a time. If the test is multiple-choice, try to eliminate as many choices as you can that you know are wrong. If you can narrow it down to two choices, then even if you guess, you have a 50–50 chance of being right! On a fill-in-the-blanks test, if you have some idea what the answer might be, then guess.

One tip to remember is this: often, an answer or a clue to an answer to a question may be given in a question that appears somewhere else on the test. This is another good reason to go all through the test one time before answering any questions.

If you come to a question that you just can't answer at all, don't worry. Just go on to the next question, and save the really hard ones until the end.

On essay questions, sometimes you may not know the exact answer to the question, but you may know something else that's important about the subject. Many teachers will give you part or even full credit for telling what you *do* know.

On a test, Joanne came across the question, "Who invented the cotton gin?" She didn't know the answer, but instead of leaving it blank, she wrote, "I can't remember who invented the cotton gin, but I do know that Elias Howe invented the sewing machine." The teacher gave her half-credit for her answer!

After you've answered as many questions as you can, check over your answers. Unless you are sure that an answer is wrong, don't change it. Most of the time, your first reaction is correct, so leave it alone unless you know it's wrong.

One last tip on test-taking—unless your teacher wants you to use a pen, always take a test with a pencil. And have at least one extra, sharpened pencil, and a good eraser at your desk.

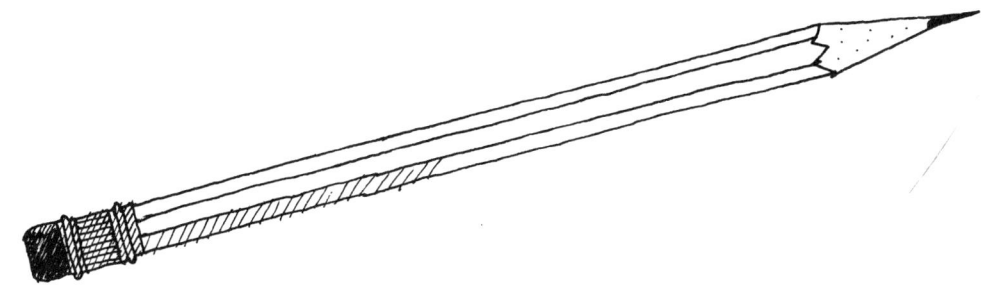

GETTING BACK THE TEST

What do you do when you get a test back? Do you look quickly at your mark, then shove the paper into your desk, never to look at it again? Or do you go over it carefully to see which questions you got right and which you got wrong, and try to figure out why?

Test results can provide you with a lot more information than simply a mark. Understanding your test results can help you understand how well you are doing, what areas you are doing well in, what areas you need to work harder in or pay more attention to.

Some teachers go carefully over each test with their classes, repeating the questions and giving the correct answers. If your teacher does this, she or he is helping students see their own strengths and weaknesses. This is valuable information, and a big help in preparing for future tests!

If your teacher does not go over the test results, you might want to suggest it to him or her. If the teacher doesn't want to take class time to go over the test results, then you can ask for a copy of the test questions, and ask your teacher to tell you the correct answers to any questions you got wrong. Or, you can look up the correct answers yourself.

A TEST IS A LEARNING ACTIVITY

A test is not just a device for measuring you or for grading you. More importantly, a test is one of the only ways that you—or your teacher—can tell how well you are understanding the things you are learning in school. If you never got weighed, it would be hard for you to tell whether you were gaining or losing weight, unless you gained or lost a lot so you couldn't help noticing. A test is the same thing—it can point out areas of difficulty before they become major problems, and can show you your own talents and skills, as well.

YOUR TEACHER IS ON YOUR SIDE

Schoolwork, homework, studying, tests—it's only scary if you feel that you and your teacher are enemies, battling each other from opposite sides of a field. The truth is, the goal of your school and your teacher is probably the same as your own—to help you gain the knowledge and skills to be independent; to let you see what there is on earth to question and explore; to encourage you to develop your own personality and talents to the fullest possible extent; and to make life better for yourself and for others now and in years to come.

THINGS TO THINK ABOUT

How do you usually feel when your teacher announces a test? Why do you think you feel this way?

Who do you think does better on a test: the student who keeps up with the daily work, or the one who leaves it all until the last minute? Why do you think this is so?

When your class has a test, do you usually cluster with the other students before the test, asking last-minute questions? Do you think this helps you and the others prepare for the test? Why or why not?

What does it mean to say that "fear is contagious"?

Why is it important to get a good night's sleep before a test? Why can being tired make you do poorly on a test?

When you get back a test, do you try to find out what you got right and what you got wrong? How can knowing these things help you?

Index

Abbreviations, 20
Asking questions, 15–16

Chapters in textbooks, 44–45
Concentration, 12–14
Cramming, 52–53

Fear, 1–2, 49, 51, 58, 59

Generalization, 39–40
Grading, 51, 59

Homework, 22
    See also Studying

Interest in subjects, 14

Learning, 5–21
    asking questions, 15–16
    concepts, 38–40
    interest in subjects, 14

    missing steps in, 10
    naming the problem, 5–6
    note-taking, see Note-taking
    paying attention, 12–14, 21
    practice, 10
    steps involved in, 6–7
    See also Studying

Memorizing, 31–37
    making sense from non-sense, 33–34
    practice, 32–33
    as problem solving, 35–36
    rules, 36
    understanding and, 35
    writing and, 20, 34, 35

Note-taking, 16–20
    organization of notes, 47
    reading and, 40, 46
    remembering and, 40–41, 46

Note-taking *(cont.)*
   tests and, 55–56

Paragraphs of textbooks, 45
Paying attention, 12–14, 21
Practice, 10
   memorizing and, 32–33
Problem solving. *See* Learning
Putting things off, 25–27

Questions, asking, 15–16

Reading, note-taking and, 40, 46
Remembering
   note-taking and, 40–41, 46
   See also Memorizing
Results of tests, 61–62
Review questions of textbooks, 45–46
Routine, 27, 28
Rules, memorizing and, 36

Schedule for studying, 27–29
Sections of textbooks, 45
Skill chart, 8
Spelling rules, 36
Steps in learning, 6–7

missing, 10
Studying, 22–30
   place for, 22, 24–25
   schedule, 27–29
   for tests, 52–53, 55–56
   time for, 25–29
Subjects, getting interested in, 14
Summaries of textbooks, 45–46

Taking notes. *See* Note-taking
Tests, 49–63
   cramming, 52–53
   day of test, 58–59
   fear of, 49, 51, 58, 59
   night before, 57
   reasons for, 51, 62
   results, 61–62
   studying for, 52–53, 55–56
   taking, 59–61
Textbooks, 44–45

Understanding, 1–4
   memorizing and, 35
Units in textbooks, 44

Writing, 6–7
   memorizing and, 20, 34, 35

About the Author

Janet Wikler lives and works in New York City. A *cum laude* graduate of the University of Pennsylvania, Ms. Wikler has taught at the elementary and high school levels. More recently she has been professionally involved in publishing as a marketing specialist for educational and other materials. *How to Study and Learn* is her first book for children.